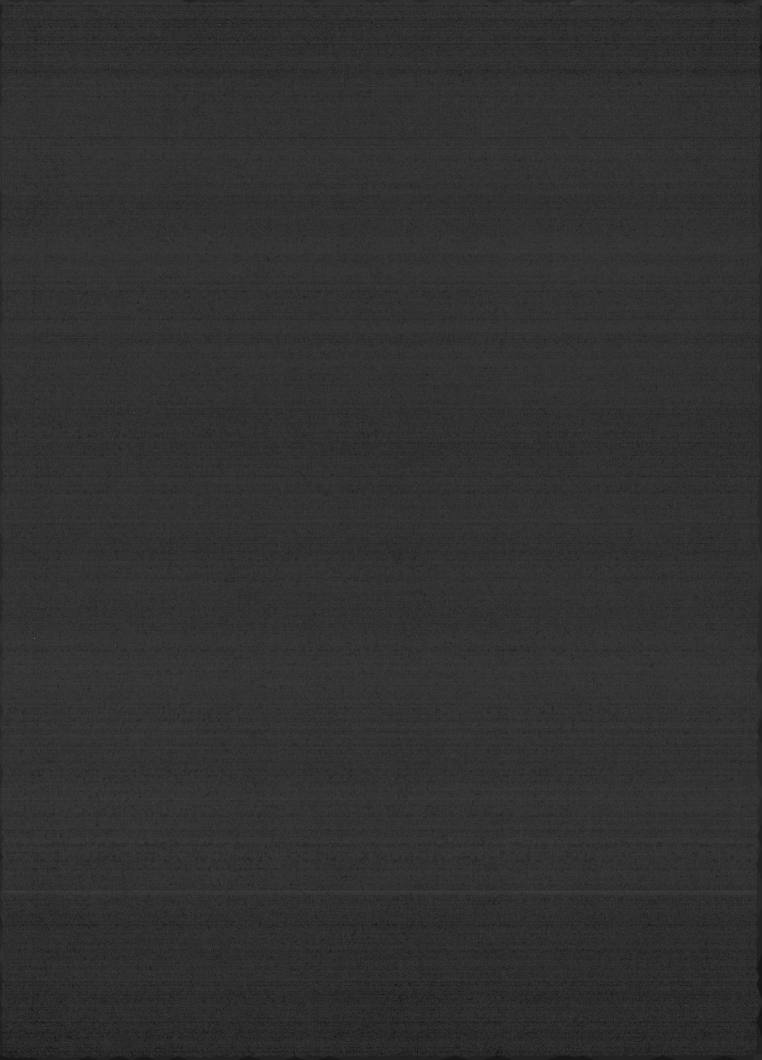

© 2023 David K

This work including all its parts is protected by copyright. Any exploitation outside the narrow limits of copyright law without the consent of the author is prohibited.

Do you have questions or concerns? Write us.
davidk.coloringbooks@gmail.com

Contact:

David K

c/o Block Services

Stuttgarter Str. 106

70736 Fellbach

Germany

Made in United States
Orlando, FL
25 October 2024